Football's All-Time Greats

HEAD COACHES

JOSH LEVENTHAL

BLACK RABBIT BOOKS

Bolt is published by Black Rabbit Books
P.O. Box 3263, Mankato, Minnesota, 56002.
www.blackrabbitbooks.com
Copyright © 2017 Black Rabbit Books

Design and Production by Michael Sellner
Photo Research by Rhonda Milbrett

Library of Congress Control Number: 2015954864

HC ISBN: 978-1-68072-039-6   PB ISBN: 978-1-68072-297-0

Printed in the United States at CG Book Printers,
North Mankato, Minnesota, 56003. PO #1796 4/16

Web addresses included in this book were working and appropriate at the time of publication. The publisher is not responsible for broken or changed links.

Image Credits

AP Images: Al Messerschmidt Archive, 12 (left), 13 (middle); ASSOCIATED PRESS, 10, 11, 12 (right), 16; Ben Margot, 26; Gene J. Puskar, Back Cover, 1, 18, 21, 27; Greg Trott, 19; John Rooney, 7; Marc Pesetsky, 12 (middle); MATT KRYGER, 24; Morry Gash, 29 (top); NFL Photos, 8, 9; Paul Spinelli, 4-5, 15; Scott Boehm, 13 (right); Scott D. Weaver, 13 (left); Getty: Jerome Davis / Contributor, Cover; Shutterstock: 22-23 (background); EKS, 3, 12-13 (background); enterlinedesign, 28-29 (bottom); grynold, 22-23 (silhouette); LABELMAN, 22-23 (silhouette); Robert Adrian Hillman, 22-23 (silhouette); Svyatoslav Aleksandrov, 31; VitaminCo, 32; Wikimedia: 25
Every effort has been made to contact copyright holders for material reproduced in this book. Any omissions will be rectified in subsequent printings if notice is given to the publisher.

Contents

Calling
the Play

The team is inches from making a touchdown. The head coach looks at his play chart. He tells his quarterback what to do. On the **sideline**, the coach watches the play closely.

Touchdown!

Coaches

from 1920 to 1965

The head coach of a football team has many jobs. He is a teacher. And he is a leader. The coach also has to make a plan for every game.

When the **NFL** started, many coaches were also players. Some owned the teams, as well.

Paul Brown

George Halas VS. Curly Lambeau

40	seasons as head coach	**33**
497	regular-season games coached	380
13–0 **(1934)**	best season record	**12–0–1** **(1929)**
6	NFL championships	**6**

George Halas and Earl "Curly" Lambeau

George Halas owned the Bears for 63 years. Halas was the first coach to hold practices every day. He was also the first to study **films** of other teams.

Curly Lambeau started the Packers in 1919. He coached until 1949. And he played quarterback for years too. Lambeau used **passing** plays more than other coaches.

Paul Brown

Paul Brown coached the Cleveland Browns for 16 years. He started a way of coaching that continues today. He hired a **staff** to help him. He also started calling plays from the sideline.

Vince Lombardi

Vince Lombardi coached the Packers for nine seasons. He pushed players to be the best. With his coaching, the team won the first two Super Bowls.

The Super Bowl trophy is named after Lombardi.

CAREER COACHING RECORDS (through 2015)

350 — 328 318

300 —

250 — 250 226 213 223

200 — 156 148 162 132 104 113

150 —

100 —

50 — 31 22 9
6 6 0

Don Shula | George Halas | Tom Landry | **Curly Lambeau** | Paul Brown | Bill Belichick

12

WINS-LOSSES-TIES
(regular season)

	350
	300
	250
	200

193
148

139
69

104
55

96
34

92
59

92
52

	150
	100
	50

1
0
1
6
1
0

Chuck Noll · **Tony Dungy** · **Mike McCarthy** · **Vince Lombardi** · **Bill Walsh** · **Mike Tomlin**

CHAPTER 3

Coaches

from 1966 to 1999

The late 1960s through the 1990s were a time of change. Coaches created new plays for **offenses**. Passing became a bigger part of the game. Coaches found new ways to use **defenses** too.

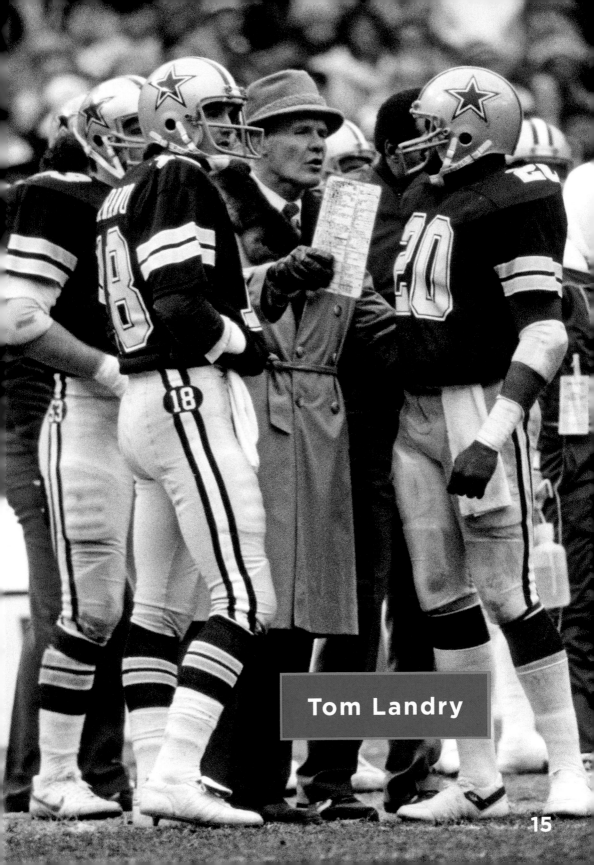

Tom Landry

Coaches with Longest Careers with One Team

Tom Landry

29

seasons with Cowboys

• • • • • Don Shula and Tom Landry

No NFL coach won more games than Don Shula. Including **play-off** games, he won 347 times. He coached in six Super Bowls.

Tom Landry was the first coach of the Cowboys. Landry's team played in five Super Bowls. He was known for trying new plays. Many of his plays are still used today.

Curly Lambeau	Don Shula	Chuck Noll
29	**26**	**23**
seasons with **Packers**	seasons with **Dolphins**	seasons with **Steelers**

Bill Walsh and Chuck Noll

Bill Walsh coached the 49ers. His team used many short passes. With Walsh, the 49ers won three Super Bowls.

Chuck Noll's Steelers won four Super Bowls. He was the first coach to win that many. Noll got many of his best players in the college **draft**.

Bill Walsh

CHAPTER 4

Coaches

from 2000 to Today

Coaches use a lot of technology today. They use computers to plan plays. And they talk to players through headsets. Coaching staffs are also much bigger. Some head coaches have more than 20 assistants.

21

ASSISTANT COACHES

Teams use many assistant coaches. Each assistant has a specific job.

QUARTERBACK COACH

STRENGTH COACH
in charge of weight training

DEFENSIVE COORDINATOR
in charge of the defense

OFFENSIVE COORDINATOR
in charge of the offense

LINEBACKER COACH

SECONDARY COACH
in charge of cornerback and safeties

SPECIAL TEAMS COACH
in charge of kickers and return teams

Tony Dungy

The Colts went to the play-offs every season with Tony Dungy. Dungy holds the record for making the play-offs. His team made it 10 years in a row. He also coached the Colts to a Super Bowl win.

Dungy was the first African American head coach to win a Super Bowl.

Bill Belichick

Bill Belichick is head coach of the Patriots. He led the team to its first Super Bowl victory. Then he led the team to three more. Belichick is tied with Chuck Noll for most Super Bowl wins.

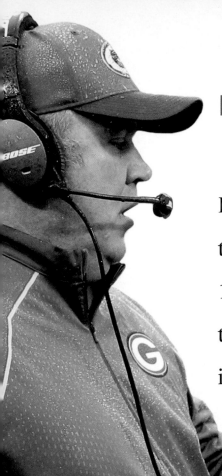

Mike McCarthy

Mike McCarthy coaches the Packers. McCarthy's team made the play-offs in eight of 10 seasons. He led the team to a Super Bowl win in 2010.

Mike McCarthy VS. Mike Tomlin

through 2015

Mike McCarthy		Mike Tomlin
10	seasons as head coach	**9**
160	games coached	144
15–1	best regular-season record	12–4
1–0	Super Bowl record	**1–1**
8-7	play-off win-loss record	**6-5**

Mike Tomlin

Mike Tomlin's Steelers won the
Super Bowl in 2008. He is the youngest
head coach ever to win a Super Bowl.

Leading to Win · · · · · · · · · ·

Head coaches are the leaders of football teams. They are praised for wins. They are blamed for losses. Teams need coaches to push them to get better.

Timeline

1915

October 1929
Great Depression begins

September 1939
World War II begins

1919
Curly Lambeau
starts the Packers.

July 1969
first moon landing

September 2001
terrorist attack on World
Trade Center and Pentagon

1979
Chuck Noll
is first coach
to win four
Super Bowls.

1995
Don Shula
wins 347th
game.

2006 season
Tony Dungy is first
African American coach
to win a Super Bowl.

2008 season
Mike Tomlin is
youngest coach
to win a
Super Bowl.

2015

GLOSSARY

defense (DEE-fens)—the players on a team who try to stop the other team from scoring

draft (DRAFT)—a system in which new players are chosen for professional teams

film (FILM)—a video recording

NFL—short for National Football League

offense (AW-fens)—the group of players in control of the ball trying to score points

passing (PAS-ing)—throwing

play-off (PLAY-ahf)—a series of games played after the regular season to decide which player or team is the champion

sideline (SIYD-liyn)—a line that marks the outside edge of a sports field or court

staff (STAF)—a group of people who work for an organization or business

BOOKS

Anastasio, Dina. *What Is the Super Bowl?* What Was ...? New York: Grosset & Dunlap, 2015.

Cosson, M. J. *Superstars of the Green Bay Packers.* Pro Sports Superstars. Mankato, MN: Amicus, 2014.

Jacobs, Greg. *The Everything Kids' Football Book: All-Time Greats, Legendary Teams, and Today's Favorite Players.* Everything Kids' Series. Avon, MA: Adams Media, 2014.

WEBSITES

Famous Coaches
www.biography.com/people/groups/coaches

Football: Strategy
www.ducksters.com/sports/footballstrategy.php

Pro Football Hall of Fame
www.profootballhof.com

INDEX